GW00660126

with love

Kate
Julet x

K TeA

A lot of Positivi-Tea
has been drunk and
spilt in the

making of
this book......

Turning Tides

Kate Tulett

Thankyou to all my friends, family and the rats and rascals who support me daily. Special thanks to the person who inspired me to write this book and to many others who kept me going.

Having studied Design & Technology at Leeds Metropolitan University, she has worked as an art teacher at many schools and colleges across the country and is currently head of art at a Surrey school.

Kate's passion is textiles and mixed media, and she loves to encourage students to experiment with all-sorts of materials. She uses reclaimed, recycled materials wherever possible and her frames are reused and up-cycled from discarded frames or made from reclaimed wood.

During Covid Kate opened up a workshop and studio to enable her to have a creative space to grow and produce her art. Since 2020 Kate has expanded her business and runs art courses, clubs, workshops for 5 - 500yr olds!

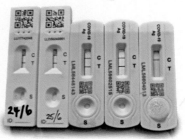

Just when you're about to give up on me,
the tide turns and you see my
true potential.

Introduction

My head was absolutely battered. I was turning 50. I felt lost, breathless, choked, frustrated. I thought "I am an artist, how can I fix my head, myself?"

This was my answer. I hope it gives just one of you as many thought provoking moments as it did me making it!

The work I did in covid was dark and angry because I was so frustrated and it was a way for me to express myself. So after 2 years of feeling controlled and feeling like I was encased in a straight jacket, I needed liberating.

2022 was the year I was 50 and I wanted to do something to both celebrate and commemorate it.

I have always wanted to do some sort of art book. So I put the idea out there to the world of social media friends for suggestions, "What do I do? 52 cold swims, 52 walks (already done that) 52 this, 52 that. But one stood out 52 appreciations and to illustrate them. So here they are all 52 (53 if you count the front cover as I hate even numbers) A whole year of life's learning, accepting, appreciating and trying to live the big and not so big events of 2022.

Hope you enjoy it as much as I enjoyed making it!

Kate x

1.

'Insight'

'Thank you for opening my eyes and heart,
because to be who you truly are, you have to
accept what you feel deep within your soul.'

This is my metaphorical eye. The eyes of a person give them away, I think that's where the phrase 'The eyes are the windows to the soul' comes from. I'm thanking the universe for allowing me to see things more clearly. For showing me how to look within and see myself. I am authentic, quirky and wear my heart on my sleeve.

I have come such a long way on my own personal journey of self-discovery as a person and as an artist. This is why now I feel I can make this book. But I'm ever the pupil, I'm still learning. I need to learn to appreciate people, places and things more and not take them for granted.

2

'Got me Tea'

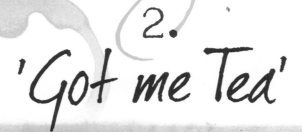

Appreciate the
small things
cup of tea
By the Sea
That'll do me

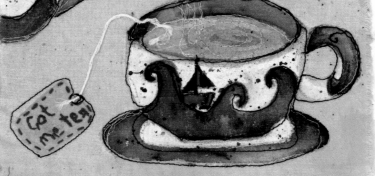

Got me tea

kate Tulett 2022

cup of
tea by the Sea

It's very clear to everyone around me, those who see my work and those who own pieces, how much I love the sea. I am calmed and grounded by the sea. It feeds my creativity and my soul. My work is all about the sea, everything I do is usually influenced by it one way or another. I love its unpredictability, its power, its strength, its calmness, I love its hidden secrets and furious storms that destroy everything in its path yet leaving treasures on the beach for us to find and to make into art. I love it, it's part of me, it calls me when I need it. I can sit staring at it for hours, drinking a cup of tea whilst soaking up its powerful energy. I'm sure in a previous life I was a fish.

'Appreciate the small things –
Cup of tea, by the sea,
that'll do me.'

11

Got me tea!

3.
'Joy'

Even the rats
and rascals
In my life can
Bring me joy

'Even the rats and rascals in
my life can bring me joy'

I am a big kid as a teacher. When I was at school I was a challenge. Having undoubtedly undiagnosed ADHD because I grew up in the eighties. I was a lively, loud, messy, annoying, talkative, eccentric little girl with the nick name of 'floating Annie' yet I was a 'thorn' in my French teacher's side (according to my teacher on parents evening). But I loved school. A hub of excitement, no two days ever being the same, its own little community of children. It's one of the biggest reasons I love teaching. I know I'm good at it and I absolutely love it. The children are the best thing about the job, their inquiring minds, their keenness to learn, their adaptability and their naive, honest opinions. Although most days I have children that literally drive me insane and never leave me alone. They want to be in my classroom at every single opportunity they can. They are the rats and rascals in my life, and I would not have it any other way.

Covid stole my classroom and closed the doors of clubs and extras, and I didn't realise how much I missed it until it happened. Not being able to sit amongst the children and chat, show them how to do things, banter about the small things. So when covid began to leave us and we opened back up as a country, I swore I would always allow a space for the child to be able to come, a safe place for some to come and work, others just to find that quiet (or not so quiet) space. I don't have and have never had favourites, although the students would tell you that each one of them believes that they are my favourite. I even have them writing on my whiteboard in my classroom in order of who is my favourite, and someone always rubs out the name at the top to write their own name. And that, in itself, is why at 50 I am still in teaching.

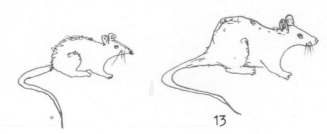

4. 'Eunice'

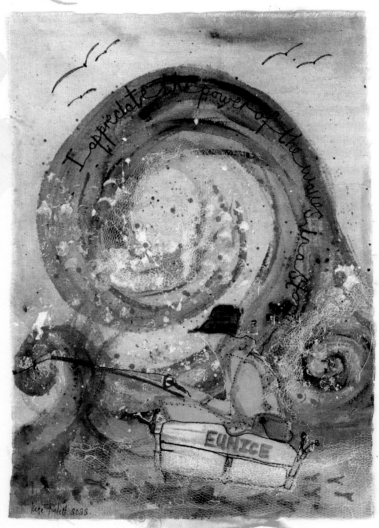

'I appreciate the power of the
waves in a storm.'

This is the week of the huge storm Eunice, she came, she caused carnage and she left. Still, we go on, we go on our merry way doing whatever we are doing and happily oblivious to the world around us. That's me living in my bubble of art and teaching every day. Something happens, but we just put our heads down and march forwards and onwards.

I sometimes see myself like a storm. I grow, I bubble up, I explode then its calm again. My head is clear, and I move on. I see a storm like a reset, it washes away the things that need to go, it clears the head. This is most definitely when the sea is at its most beautiful, powerful and most of all majestic. The humongous waves crashing and destroying everything in its wake. This is my favourite kind of sea to watch, I'm in utter awe it is amazing.

5. 'Mine'

Always appreciate what you have before it becomes something you had x

mine Mine mine

'Always appreciate what you have before it becomes something you had!'

Why are some humans just so selfish? They really don't
see the bigger picture, they can't see what they have,
right in front of them. Why do people always want more,
more, more? Greed is an evil quality in people. Like
the whole toilet roll thing during covid. I don't know
whether covid exacerbated greed, but my goodness we
as humans are so selfish. People have become more
entitled. 'I'm entitled to because'. This reasoning
enrages me. Before I went into recovery, when I was
destroying myself any way I could, I could not see the
carnage I was leaving in my wake. I was so focussed
on my own issues in my own little world that I didn't
notice anybody else's. I wasn't aware of the impact
of my actions, I was hurting everyone else around me
because I believed the whole world owed me a favour.
Oh, how wrong I was, and it's times like this week when
I look at how far I have come, and now I see how selfish
some people really are or is it how self-centred and
unkind some people have become? To me you have to
be kind, to treat people how you want to be treated
yourself. If you are kind you receive
kindness, because karma comes
and gets you in the end.

MINE

6.

'War Paint'

Appreciate your
Freedom
because you can!

WAR PAINT

This week it was suggested that all the women and children were to leave the Ukraine due to possible war starting in Ukraine with Russia. Why is it always the case that people must leave their families for war, it's upsetting and it's sad. It's like they must grieve because they may not see these people again. Who chooses to stay and fight? We, here in the UK have only ever experienced not seeing our families in recent times of covid and that was bad enough. And as the war is beginning so soon after covid restrictions. It's horrendous how people are being pulled away from their loved ones once again. So this is a week of reflection, I reflect on how lucky we are to have our own freedom. The poor women who are putting on a brave face for their families and are standing strong and leaving their loved ones behind to fight. It is so profound for these people to do this, and for that I applaud them.

'Appreciate your freedom because you can!'

7. 'Strength'

A woman is like a tea bag, you never know how strong she is until she gets into hot water.

This week I struggle with being divorced.
Divorce is hard for everyone who is involved.
You try to do it amicably and you try to please
people and try not to lose every penny you
have to the solicitors who are in the middle.
I work 2 jobs, 3 if you count trying to sell my
own art. It's really, really, really hard to
pay for things, always feeling like my head is
just above the water financially. And then you
get hit by a curve ball and the money doesn't
come. Your head at this point drops below the
water, you're holding your breath until you
can breathe again. It's full of ups and downs,
but still we go on, still we put up the pretence
that everything is OK to the child that you
love who is caught in the middle. The buck
stops with me. I am plan A, plan B
and plan C. Shout out to all you
single people doing exactly
the same.

'A woman is like a teabag:
you never know how strong she is
until she gets into hot water.'

8.

'Lightbulb Moment'

LIGHTBULB MOMENT

Being a teacher doesn't just mean inspiring children, it's about...

Being a teacher doesn't just mean inspiring children, it's also about how they inspire you too. I absolutely love teaching children, they inspire me every day, they make me laugh out loud daily and most of all they are my best advisors. They don't judge you and they seem to see you for who you really are warts and all. Their opinion matters to me more than some of the adults in my life. They give me an honest answer when asked for one, whether I like it or not. Especially about my art, even giving suggestions to make it better. Their ideas are new and fresh.

At 50 finding fresh and new ideas can be quite tricky. I always seem to find a little group of advisors that are always around to ask for advice for ideas for new topics and the fact that I trust their responses encourages better ideas.

'Being a teacher doesn't just mean inspiring children, it's about how they inspire you too.'

9.
'Words of Wisdom'

'Appreciate the advice given from
people that love you.'

WISDOM

In life I try to avoid listening to advice as
sometimes I can take it as criticism. But to
move forwards you need to hear it. Sometimes
if I hear the same advice enough, from
various sources, I then accept it and begin to
believe it. I can find it hard because I used
to be very self-critical, and I find it hard
to articulate what I want to say. Which is why
I do it in art. This week I actually took the
advice and moved forward from something
I had completely misunderstood. So, this WISDOM
week I'm appreciating the words of wisdom
that were spoken to me as I clearly needed a
little word in my ear to let it go.

WISDOM

10.

'Emotion'

'Learning to appreciate that when it all gets
a little too much you need to take a break.'

COVID, I absolutely detest it. I hate it.
It nearly sent me completely mad in lockdown,
totally and utterly mad. My emotions were
literally like the sea in this appreciation,
unpredictable, powerful, strong, and dark.
I worked as a teacher all the way through
covid, online and in the school. I started a
business and have not taken time to myself
unless it has been forced upon me. This week
it is forced upon me again, covid rears its
ugly head within me, my body screaming
to me to stop, slow down, take a break and
I ignore it. I keep going, then I break, it
forces me to stop. And for that I'm actually,
really grateful. It gave me time to stop and
rejuvenate again. I must take the time to
heal and feel 100%. I refer to it as being like
the sea because I feel like a capsized boat
in a storm adrift, it has its ups and downs. I
really should listen to my body more. I tell
myself next time will be different.

11.

'Love life'

Today I appreciate 6 years of sobriety

'Today I celebrate 6 years of sobriety

SOBRieTy

This week I appreciate 6 years of sobriety.
What is sobriety?
Why do we celebrate it?

Sobriety refers to the psychological and physical logical state of being affected by the presence of an intoxicant. Basically, living a life free of any substance that is addictive, like caffeine, sugar, alcohol, and drugs. On this day 6 years ago, I underwent a life changing operation which was intended to help me with being overweight. But what it really did was mind blowingly amazing. The fact is today, although not perfect, it doesn't matter why I did it anymore, because it made me re-evaluate my life, get off my ledge and carry on stronger and braver. Sometimes we just need to stop and look at ourselves through the eyes of others.

I am lucky I got that chance to do that, I never want to go back to this, I am starting to like who I am now and these moments remind me how far I have come. Like finding my pot of gold at the end of my own rainbow from one of my storms. And for that I am eternally grateful.

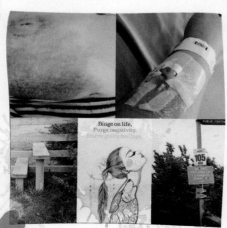

12.

'Bunny'

'To appreciate a lovely reminder of how
beautiful change can really be'

Bluebells, I love them. I love the colour.
I love the smell and probably because in
abundance they look remarkably like the sea.
A sea of bluebells!

This year they are particularly brilliant,
and I got to see them both here in Surrey and
in Yorkshire. Bluebells are the one flower
that I have painted nearly all my artistic
life. I have used them in lots of artwork.
Truly beautiful bluebells that smell so
lovely. I love it when the dogs sit in them,
the children run through them, and people
travel miles and miles and miles to see them.
They are there in abundance this week.
It really is a wonderful reminder that better
days are coming, lighter nights, warmer
days and a fabulous reminder of just how
beautiful change can really be.
And we should embrace change more
rather than fear it.

13. 'Bee Kind'

I think that kindness breeds kindness. Even when I feel angry with people, I still find that treating them with kindness sometimes has the most profound effect.

I once had a student that I was not looking forward to teaching, because of their behaviour and reputation in the year below. I started to teach them, but I thought if I sit them next to me and be really kind and loving towards them, it would be OK. And what happened was really quite amazing.

They became a huge asset in the classroom and what was even better was that they grew to absolutely love art in the process. So, this week if I try being kind to somebody, it will reap its rewards. Out of fear and dread can come the most beautiful gift of all.

'Sometimes you just need to be kind!'

14. 'Fragile'

Appreciating the freedom that comes from their strength ♥

I find my life is a balancing act. I am a teacher, a single parent, an artist, and owner of a successful business, and at times I don't know whether I am coming or going. When one of these things is off kilter, then it can send me a little over the edge. Everything is fine when they are all working in sync and alongside each other. But when one, only one, needs more attention than the others, it becomes a very fine line of sanity. This is where I must draw from my reserves, from my core and find my inner strength. Knowing it's only temporary and won't last forever and knowing that I will survive it, comforts me. I've survived worse, and I will survive this. This is also when I make some of my best artwork. I am fragile, although you may not see me as that, but that is enough.

'Appreciate the freedom that comes from inner strength."

15. 'Survivor'

Appreciating that we are able to provide a place for those who seek refuge ♡

This week one of my closest friends took in a young refugee girl from the Ukraine. For the past few months she, along with others had been hiding in a church basement, frightened, unsure and alone, in fear for their life. We, as a country, are very lucky to be able to provide others in need of a home. I am very proud of my friend and her family, who have given their time and support to this refugee. Taking in a complete stranger is a brave and courageous thing to do and I absolutely applaud them for doing so. We are all trying to do our bit. I am eternally grateful for being able to do my bit too by supporting then throughout.

'Appreciating that we are able to provide a place for those who seek refuge.'

16. 'Tedious'

learning to appreciate how time consuming report writing is....

Writing reports is one of the most time-consuming jobs for a teacher. When you teach every child across 4-year groups and need to report how everyone is doing, in detail, in such a short time scale is tedious especially for me who finds it hard to write and would much prefer to talk and show the parents their books of artwork. I try to give each child my individual attention, so I have to step out of my comfort zone write in a language I'm not used to (professional not casual) I talk to my students weekly. I prefer this to marking, talking to them. It's a job that has to be done every year and has had for the past 25 years of teaching. You'd think it gets easier, but it doesn't. But head down and on we go. The satisfaction and relief when you finish them is quite euphoric and for that I am very happy indeed. Every year I say I'll start them sooner too. *Hmmmmmm*

'Learning to appreciate how time-consuming report writing is.'

17. 'Being Exposed'

'Learning to appreciate our vulnerability
in today's society'

This week a group of teenagers shared a photo of me. They had found it online from over 7 years ago; maybe more.

It was when I was in a bad place mentally and physically. I had never seen that photo before. They shared the photo amongst the year group and had a laugh at my expense.

I was angry and upset that these young kids who were 'having a laugh' took me back to a dark and horrible place, they made me feel vulnerable, exposed, violated. It was a part of me that I wanted to forget.

For the first time in my 25 years as a teacher I wanted to quit and run and hide.

Somehow from doing this appreciation, I picked myself up, held my head high and forgave. The anger and shame dissipated and I remembered to be grateful that I am not that person anymore, I've grown, I've learned, I've changed.

I also had a little giggle as I thought to myself. Thank f**k they didn't have social media in the 90's, it could have been much worse.

18.
'Life'

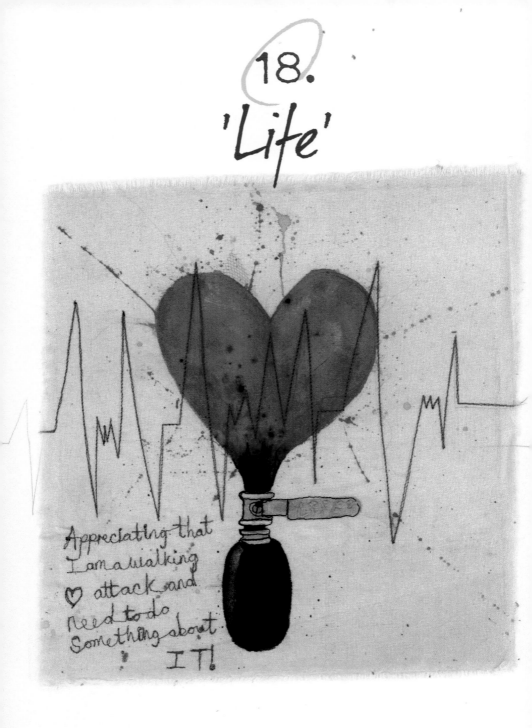

Appreciating that I am a walking ♡ attack and need to do something about IT!

I battle with my health over and over again. It becomes part of me and my daily routine. But this week I was bad. I could not get my blood pressure down.

I know I need to lose a bit (well a lot) of weight but I'm happy in my own skin. I'm not in the headspace I once was and now being older. and wiser maybe'. I now worry about looking a lot older, and if I lost the weight all that saggy skin would now not retract and I'd look like a deflated camel.

Getting my blood pressure checked is a priority, I felt really scared, I know I need to sort it out.

Doing this appreciation made me think I need to get my arse into gear. Loving life as a larger person is ok. I am who I am.

'Appreciating that I am a walking heart attack and need to something about it'

It's the Jubilee. This week we celebrate 75 years of the Queen on the throne. 75 years doing the same job. It's really quite strange to think how much life has changed in that time. 75 years ago, there were no phones, no laptops, no sky tv, no social media and now we reflect on how much the world has really changed in her reign. The quote I used here is really quite profound because the Queen spoke the words."History was not made by those who did nothing".

'History was not made by those who did nothing.'
(Queen Elizabeth II)

20.
'Cricket'

Appreciating cricket

Never give up—absolutely never give up

This week I am appreciating the sport of cricket with a quote by Shane Warne, one of the best cricketers of all time, he said 'Never give up, no matter absolutely never give up!' As the cricket season starts again in our house, I never really appreciated how good the game was before I met and lived with a cricketer. I have grown to love it really and it isn't as boring as I once believed. It's a time of reflection, it's a time of skill and it's a time for endurance to stay out all day, playing the game for the entire day, sometimes five days in a row. As a player you really need some grit or you have to pull on your inner strength to play the game, you have bad days and good days and sometimes it really is in the last over, that a game can be won or lost. Just like the title of this book 'Turning Tides' just when you think all is lost and the game is over the tide turns and it changes instantly. So that's why you should never give up, absolutely never give up on anything worth doing!

'Appreciating cricket, by never giving up, absolutely never giving up!

(Shane Warne)

21. 'Rage'

'No words.'

No Words can write how I actually felt. So I draw a raging silent scream a reflection of my inner self all of this week. This weekend I was humiliated so badly that I really was taken aback. I had no words to describe how I felt. I responded by just walking away and leaving. Sometimes when you have an awful lot to say a lot of the time, silence is your power. I don't think I have ever quite felt like this before, I had worked so hard on a project for a fundraiser only to be humiliated in front of the very people I was doing it for. The 'old' me never walked away. I would fight and argue. I felt so small. I didn't know that people could make me feel like this anymore and as an adult it really hurt.

It really could have turned my life completely upside down and it did for hours and hours. The longest night of my life. But once again doing an appreciation, really did take the power of the humiliation away. Every stroke of paint I painted made it better and adding the final bit of glitter to the lips gave me back my power. Oh how this girl loves glitter, and if glitter showed up more in books there would be more in this one. The rage inside me has once again subsided but the hurt is still there, but only a glimmer. But I move forward again, leave it behind on the fabric and move on.

22.
'Best Art Space'

'To appreciate being
appreciated.'

Absolutely blown away this week. To win an
award of this magnitude is unbelievable. To
all the people who voted for me to become a
winner of a Muddy Stilettos award for 2022
'Best Art space in Surrey'. Beating so many
great spaces and competition. It's truly mind
blowing. For everyone to have voted for me,
to be appreciated like this after such a bad
week last week is absolutely amazing,
restores my faith a little. I'm absolutely
gutted I couldn't collect the award in person,
but my friend and colleague who I couldn't
run this business without, went on my behalf.
Thank you to every single person for voting
for me, I could not be more grateful.

to appreciate someone who doesn't get appreciated much

#easyJet

Kd Tulett 2022

The media controlling our lives has become quite overwhelming in recent times, whipping us up in a frenzy about one thing or another. Scaremongering us about news and events. This week an airline that in recent times has received a lot of bad press, were the only ones available to help us out of a very sticky situation. The first holiday for two and a half years was almost lost due to a cancelled flight. When we booked it, we went with a company we thought wouldn't have these issues, yet they let us down. So we looked around and were saved by the one company that had the worst press at the time. It just confirms to me not to believe everything I read or see. This appreciation is dedicated to the workforce of that company and the inspiration for the appreciation was taken from their cabin crew ties. I loved them, the intertwining of the planes I thought was very appropriate for this very purpose.

'To appreciate someone who doesn't get appreciated very often.'

24. 'Tranquillity'

to appreciate the
Tranquility
Need of a holiday

Oh, the need for a holiday! I seriously underestimated how much I needed this. After a pandemic that nearly broke my spirit I needed a break.

My partner bought me it for my special birthday. He clearly could see how much I/we needed it. This year I did something I've never even thought of doing before and stayed on a boat. I've never stayed on a boat before for a holiday. It was just perfect. Quiet, calm and surprisingly still. It was idyllic, just lying about listening to the wildlife, the fish nibbling the bottom of the boat, seagulls flying above us, the boat slightly rocking in the water, it was like I was constantly meditating. That, and with the warmth of the sun on my face, who could ask for anything more? It was all I had forgotten I needed and more. Sun, sea and tranquillity. The artwork used to make the appreciation is inspired by an artist here on Lanzarote. I painted it on the beach, using the sea to clean my brushes and to add water to the paints, whilst my partner snorkelled around the bay. Perfect, absolutely perfect, here's to the next one already.

"To appreciate the need for a holiday."

25. 'Powerful'

Appreciat... that ... doesn't care how much you know until he knows how much you can...

Horses, oh does my daughter love horses. These gigantic beasts. They are powerful, majestic, intuitive and some of the most beautiful creatures on the planet. But, oh my goodness are they difficult to paint. I'll never quite master a 'Stubbs'.

Equine therapy has been found to reduce people's blood pressure and heart rate and to help calm physical symptoms of conditions of anxiety and stress, it worked for me!

These gentle giants have a very calming effect that is magnified by their size and empathy. Horses are also known for attuning themselves to human emotions often reflecting the behaviours of those around them. Having a horse to loan in covid I think helped my daughter come to terms with the isolation it created in her life, being allowed to have a relationship and see the horse, kind of made up for not physically seeing her friends. Horses genuinely don't care how much you know about them, but they do know how much you care, which is exactly why this week I wanted to pay tribute to them. Having just watched how much progress my daughter has made on her horse tonight, it reminds me of how grateful we are to have this opportunity to have the loan of an amazing horse.

'Appreciating that a horse does not care how much you know until he knows how much you care.'

26.

'Friendship'

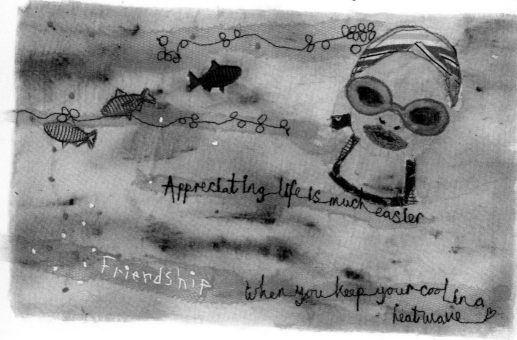

Appreciating life is much easier

Friendship

When you keep your cool in a heatwave

'Appreciating life is so much easier
when you keep your cool in a heatwave.'

Oh my goodness it is soooooooo hot. I cannot remember when it has been this hot in England and for this long. I like it like this but, at the same time it's just too hot today. I have been exceptionally lucky to be able to spend the day in a friend's pool. It reminded me of when I was a little girl in Yorkshire when all we had was a hosepipe in the garden to run through. My brother, sister and I had so much fun doing that. The kids from the local area would also come over and run through the sprinklers too. So many happy memories of family life in Yorkshire as a child in the 70's.

It was just what I needed in this heat wave. Friends are so important to me. I don't have too many best friends. I lost a few in covid due to not being able to see them, we drifted apart. Some who I couldn't live without or couldn't live without seeing have become better friends for it. Being there for each other when no one was allowed to be there for anyone was more important than I ever knew before. The friends, partner, and family I have in my life now are so precious. I appreciate them more than I can express.

Life is so much easier when you find a way to keep your cool in a heated situation.

27. 'Alice'

'Appreciating the serenity you get from walking in the woods.'

I remember when I first got my dog, my ex-husband said 'you know you do have to walk a dog!' yes, I thought, that's why I want one, to get me out of this house and walk! Little did I know that it would trigger a completely new beginning for me. One where I wanted to walk hundreds of miles, and ended up doing all sorts of walks for charity, including on my first sobriety birthday where I walked all the way round the Isle of Wight in 24 hours and 12 minutes. I found it gave me freedom and made me relate to my life's ups and downs whilst walking. I absolutely love walking, especially with my walking buddies, my dogs. The peace and quiet is so calming. It fills me with serenity, especially when I walk them in the woods first thing in the morning, The silence and stillness with no other soul around gives me the calm I need to start the day. It also gives me the time to reflect and plan my day. This week I dedicate my appreciation to one of my best friends' dog Alice, who sadly passed away this week. My friends walking companion. Oh, how these creatures touch our souls

Walking in the woods

28.

'Finding Inspiration'

Appreciating having the time to be creative.

Finding Inspiration

PAINT

School holidays are the only real time I genuinely ever really get time to have a proper break. I have time to create more art as I have more space in my head to do it. When all the hustle and bustle settles and when I take an actual break, it gives me an opportunity to do what I like best and go to the beach. It is the best place to blow the cobwebs away, and as a lot of my artwork is based on water, the sea and movement, it is where I come for ideas. I feel every now and again the sea calls out to me and I must go down to the sea to rejuvenate my soul. Like one of my favourite poems I've used lines from of over and over in my work 'Sea-Fever' by John Masefield.

'Appreciating the time to be creative.'

29.
'Fur Babies'

'I am learning to appreciate that some things fill your heart without trying.'

One of the best things I ever did was buy a schnauzer and the next best thing I did was by another. They are absolutely the best, most gentle, kind and beautiful natured dogs in the universe. I love both of my fur babies so much; they make my heart whole. They inspire me daily with their gentle nature and little quirks. I remember when we first got Betty, she was just the cutest little thing, a bundle of absolute joy. I have walked Betty and now Mabel every single day I have had them. They make my life worth living in some of my darkest days, listen intently to my ramblings with no judgement and hug me in moments of need. I am utterly blessed with these two girls in my life and it's an absolute pleasure and honour to be their life guardian.

DOGS

30. 'Dreamland'

*'Always appreciate the gift of life.
Be happy and have fun.'*

My daughter is fifteen this week. For her birthday we have gone to Margate. To 'Dreamland' for fun fun fun. 15 rides for 15 years at Dreamland must be the way to go.

I always try to do something really special for my girl's special day. Having a child for me was an absolute gift. It's giving the gift of life to another person. As a teacher I love children, otherwise why would I do the job I do? Although parenting is so different to teaching, it has its challenges and its rewards, it is absolutely the best part of being alive. I know that I am the most embarrassing mother in the world and sometimes the worst thing to ever walk the planet. But, I absolutely love this 'Pickle' and would do anything for her. Not sure that right now she loves me as much as I do her, but we are open and honest with each other and I will always be there for her whenever she needs me. No matter how bad it gets, I always want to be able to be there for her and if I can't, we will find a way together to get through it. I wish she could see her potential through my eyes, but that will only happen, I hope, when she has children of her own. I tell her this on a daily basis, and one day it will sink in. I really do love my Boo. She is absolutely the best thing that I have ever made.

31.
'Tea Time'

'Always appreciate that there is always
time for a good cup of tea.'

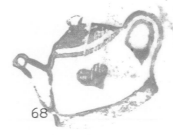

Who doesn't just love a cup of tea?
This week we went back up to
Yorkshire for a few days and
one of my favourite things to
do is to go to 'Betty's' in
Northallerton. I went with my mum and brother.
He just returned from doing an 'Ironman' oh my
God I'm too old for that sort of thing I thought!
I remember when I was doing my walks of
endurance but I'm past that now. So, to catch up
was lovely. I do so love of cup of tea. especially
at Betty's. A proper Yorkshire cup of tea. Many
a chat and world solving problems happen over
a cup of tea. Yet wars have started because of it
and also whilst at a tea party (The Boston Tea
Party). This year I have had my own set of mugs
made, for my tea at the shop, with all my little
quotes on the outside of them. Made by a fabulous
lady I work with. Quotes like 'Got me tea' (said in
a Yorkshire accent of course), 'Art is not what
you see, but what you make others sea' (DEGAS)
'Artist at work' and 'There is no such thing as a
mistake!', 'A cup of positive-TEA' and 'Art 4 All'.

32. 'New Beginnings'

'I appreciate that every day
is a new beginning.'

September is upon us and the new school year is here. As someone that has always been in Education (46 years to be exact) it's the beginning again. My new year. Each year I can start again. On the way to school, this particular morning, I saw three deer in a field. Fresh, alert, awake and ready for the day. I love going back to school after the summer holidays because everything is 'New'. New shoes, new uniform, new stationary (my absolute favourite), new bag, new academic year and a new start. I think that's why as a teacher that went straight from school to university and then straight back into school, September is my January. My resolutions are always done here, my head sees a year from September to September in a circle, always has. So my resolutions are at always made at the end of August and this years ones are;

1 Not to get behind in reports
   (Every year I say this)

2 Keep my art spaces clear. A clear space means a clear head *(Every year I start well and end diabolically lol)*

3 Plan every single lesson on google classroom, *(Actually achievable)*

4 Keeping myself to myself *(LOL)*

5 Focus on the now!! *(New one)*

33. 'Elizabeth'

HM Queen Elizabeth II

HM Queen Elizabeth II
1926 - 2022.

This week the Queen died. 75 years as our Queen.
She has died, it's not unexpected but still weird.
I'm not sure how I feel either to be honest. I really
felt the pain when Diana died. It had more of an
impact on me. I have all sorts of weird feelings
around the fact that Charles will be King now
too. Elizabeth became the Queen because of an
abdicating King. Was Charles given that option
when he wanted to marry Camilla all those years
ago? Why did he marry lady Diana? Who is to blame
or is it just fate's hand. I lived in the Diana years,
I went to see the flowers when she died, it really
upset me at the time, yet now the Queen has died.
It is very sad but I feel nothing. Maybe it's her
age and it's just the course of nature and time.
Elizabeth did only good things and for the greater
good, and served her people to the very end of her
life, like she promised us she would.

34. 'Blue'

Blue

'Always appreciate that if you are not
playful that you are not alive.'

I've always wanted a black cat, but each time I've
gone to get a cat I've either got a black and white
one because the black one has gone or I've fallen
in love with one regardless of colour. I even tried
cat protection as black cats seem to be the ones
no-one wants to adopt, but each rescue I have gone
to gives the same answer. They will not let you take
a cat if you have other pets, or children. So this
year, after I lost my two older cats I got my wish,
'Loki'. He's a little monkey, we were going to call
him Blue (like my appreciation) but soon realised
that his eyes would change colour as he got
older. He jumps, fights, bites and throws himself
everywhere, It's a cheeky little wotsit. You never
know if he's going to lick you or bite you, we named
him after Thor's brother, Loki, who in the films
we never know if he's going to play good or bad
character. After years and years of being a total
nomad after university, 13 houses in 10 years, the
first signs of actually putting roots down was
getting two cats and buying a flat. Archie and
Lexy, legends to this day they were and now I have
a whole menagerie of animals that all seem to
gravitate to the bedroom each night and keep us
company. I clearly needed a little more mischief
and light entertainment in my life, so welcome to
our home Loki.

35.
'The Queue'

'Appreciating the British public's patience and resilience they have to create 'The Queue'.

The 'queue' or the other name given to it 'The Elizabeth line' was the nickname for a queue of mourners who waited to file past the coffin of Queen Elizabeth II while she lay in state at Westminster in London England. The queue had a length of up to 10 miles and a maximum waiting time of up to 24 hours. The media commented on the significance of the queue as a symbol of the relationship the British people had to their monarch.

Could I queue for 24 hours? Absolutely not! Would I have liked to have queued for 24 hours? Yes, I would! As time had gone by and watching it all unfold on TV, I have begun to feel things. I've walked hundreds of miles at once in my time. I once walked all the way round the Isle of Wight in one go, that was gruelling enough. So to stand up for up to 24 hours and not sit down, no way, no how, not ever. I am full of admiration to see some of my friends, colleagues and acquaintances do it. England is famous for its queuing, so not surprised to see thousands of people patiently lining up doing it, even celebrities. It is absolutely amazing and actually quite awe inspiring especially as they waited like everyone else and didn't use their fame to their advantage (well most of them).

36. 'Turning Tides'

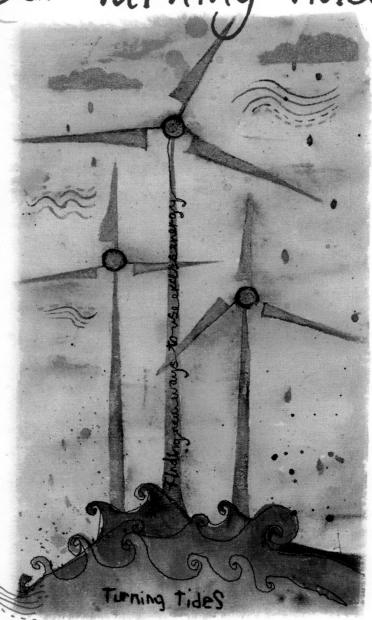

Turning tides

Finding ways to use excess energies, is hard. That is me, an undiagnosed 70's ADHD child. I never sat still or in my seat very long, I can get bored quite easily, I definitely get distracted easily and if not channelled right, or in the right way, I become a little disruptive and say inappropriate things that I haven't even thought of sometimes. I am the pain of my colleagues lives I'm sure. Though I need to learn to channel them into positive areas, instead of being obliged to sit still and listen. I still behave like a child, but am also aware that I am like it, so I do try to use my energies in things that matter. Wind turbines use the excess energy of the wind over the land and especially the sea, they are useful, making renewable energy and making it work for everyone. Some, see them as an eyesore. Not me, I love them. I'm fascinated with them, they remind me of the windmills I used to put in the garden to make it more colourful for Ariella when she was a little girl, blowing freely in the wind. I have drawn them quite a few times in my work too, especially seeing them in so much abundance these days in the sea.

I see myself as a wind turbine sometimes, spinning wildly, but if channelled right I can be an asset. Like the turning tides, just when you want to give up on me, I change direction and show you my true potential!

'Finding new ways to use excess energy'

37. 'Storm'

They Whispered to her
"You cannot withstand the storm"
"I am the storm!" she replied

This week is national poetry week. As an artist who always uses lots of different poems, quotes, and rhymes in their work, (sometimes I cannot work out who wrote them so I appologise that I can't give the credit). It's quite a powerful week. I love reading poems, I am not the world's best at English, and I try to use art to speak for me, but to help people understand just a small part of what I do, I like to include the words. This image reminds me of my daughter, no matter how many times I draw people, trace or freehand they always seem to look like or resemble her. It's like I'm stuck, I've even tried tracing faces, but no matter how much I try, male or female, they always look like either me or Ariella. Ariella is always on my mind, my only child, who didn't come with a manual (did anyone get one?) and oh do I get it wrong sometimes. I always try to own my mistakes; I will always apologise, and I've taught her to do the same. She is fierce, independent, strong and beautiful. She had wild curly hair when she was little, and I loved it. She surprises me with her own strength and is my hero. She works so hard and has her own personal challenges and she is such a hard working girl. So, to her I dedicate this appreciation with the quote that I found on a poster and do not know who originally said it 'They whisper to her, 'you cannot withstand the Storm' 'I am the storm!' she whispered back.

38. 'Headspace'

'Sticks and stones may break my bones,
but words will never hurt me.'

It's world mental health day this week and as someone who has
suffered with mental health issues for several years, I find
this both a quite personal yet a thought-provoking week. The
inspiration for this picture I found on 'Pinterest' and it's a
direct copy of the image except for the colour and the words.
I freehand machine embroidered all the words and names that I
have been called by other people, words that have been said out
loud directly towards me, words I have overheard other people say
when they think I can't hear them, words I've imagined what other
people have thought about me and words that I have used towards
myself, about myself.

'Sticks and stones may break my bones, but words will never
hurt me!' in my head is the biggest pile of crap ever said or
written. The words and names stay in my head way past the
healing of a cut or bruise, they cut deeper than any stick or
stone could, and they remain lodged in my mind. I am learning
that you can choose to let them manifest themselves, only if
you let them. You don't have to listen to them. I have found
during this time I've been making these appreciations that they
only stay in my head till I paint, draw or write them down. I
find words are used as weapons. Words can be misheard, twisted
and hurtful, but also words are expressive, profound and
complimentary too and words I often find very difficult to say.
In my art I can express a more powerful statement by drawing my
feelings rather than saying the words. Words that form from a
piece of art are personal, thought provoking and are your own.
Then words become powerful. I remain to this day a little damaged
but I am most definitely not broken.

39. 'Freedom'

I offer myself to Thee – To build with me and to do with me as thou wilt Relieve me of the bondage of self, that I may better do thy will Take away my difficulties, that victory over them may bear witness to those I would help of thy Power, thy Love, and thy Way of life

This week a good friend of mine died. Her demons got hold of her and she died. I am absolutely devastated. She held my hand at the start of my recovery and continued to do so for three years. This appreciation is dedicated to her and is called 'freedom'. It's about freeing yourself from the bondage of ones self-will, she was like a caged bird, trapped inside herself, frustrated, lost and desperate. She lost both her father and partner during covid and they were her tower of strength. Without them both she struggled to exist in everyday life. She knew that if she let her demons get hold of her that this is what would happen to her, so I have no doubt she had her eyes wide open when she picked up that first drink, that 'F**k it' button was pressed and pressed hard. She needed to get off this ferris wheel called life and go find her loved ones again. To find freedom, free once more, free from the pain, free from hurt. I'm upset and cross at the same time, but desperately wish that she would have reached out so that I could have been there for her like she was for me. Rest in peace my friend. I will forever remember her, and I will learn from her.

40.
'Mind over Matter'

'Enjoy your life no matter what is happening in the mind.'

I always have a busy head, full of ideas, full
of lists, dates to remember, appointments, jobs,
worries and plans. My head is always 'Mind Full'
trying hard to be 'mindful'. Each year I celebrate
Halloween at my art workshops. This year we
celebrated with sugar skulls. I love them and I
find that children really love them and Halloween
too. It's the only time in the year when it seems
to be appropriate to be scary and gory. This
week I also realised that I only have twelve more
appreciations left to do. My head is at bursting
point this time of the year, and sometimes I almost
feel I could break, snap into a million pieces.
Especially this week when I am still processing
the loss of my friend too. I'm learning how to
cope with losing someone like this. This is my
first friend to die and I really am struggling.
Listening to my negative thoughts really is not
very good for me so I try to turn my feelings into
something arty instead. It's a good way for me
to process my feelings and let go of those self-
sabotaging thoughts. When words fail me, my art
never does.

41. 'Emma'

'I am one at the sail,
I am the one master of my sea!'

Emma's funeral is this week and I'm finding it hard and it's an extremely sad time. Not sure why it has affected me so much, maybe because at times in covid I felt the same but I was able to shake myself out of it or focus elsewhere.

I haven't seen her for a long time, but we both followed a similar path before finding sobriety and we were very alike as people. These last couple of weeks I have had to look within myself again and again and to think about how I could have also let my demons take over my head like they did hers. At the minute I'm feeling strong and through a lot of self-reflection and taking a full moral inventory of myself and addressing my faults and I am able to move forward. My life is like an ocean, with its ups and downs, it is calm and then it is a storm, looking good on the surface but underneath all is not well, dangers lying beneath the surface. These are invisible to everyone but me. Questioning whether I am so much different from Emma. I have her fear, her panic, her anxiety about so many different things and it is hard sometimes to balance the good with the bad. It's like I'm lost at sea with no wind in my sails, losing all hope ... but again and again whist making this book I am finding that painting and writing my thoughts and feelings down, help me to turn my own tides yet again! My appreciations make me steer my own boat in the direction my own journey. It was so appropriate to dedicate this appreciation to Emma with words used from her service from the song 'Believer' by The Imagine Dragons.

42.
'Inner Beauty'

You can't go back and change the begining but you can start where you are now and change the Ending ♥

'You can't go back and change the beginning, but you can start where you are and change the ending.'

Why have I let myself get so overweight again,
am I just thinking about Emma again? Why can I
conquer almost everything else except this? Why
do people judge you on your size? People don't make
nice clothes to fit larger people. Some of the most
beautiful things are so small, they are made for
children, yet I want to wear them. I don't know what
I do wrong, well yes, I do, I eat too much. If I could
only go back in time and pinpoint why I do it I'd
go back and change it. I genuinely don't know what
happened for me to be like this. All I know is that
I love food. I don't drink anymore, I don't do drugs,
yes, I have money worries but who doesn't when they
are a single parent with 2 jobs. I guess everyone
is worried about something. I would try and fix
it, but I genuinely don't understand why. Weight
seems to be my one burden. I so aspire to look lovely
and thin, but at the same time I wonder, at what
sacrifice? The last time I tried to do this I ended
up with sepsis and nearly died. When I think back

to that now, I know that I can't
change the past in any point, and
I really don't live there anymore.
What I can do is make my own
positive choices and write my
own ending to move forward.

43. 'The Shard'

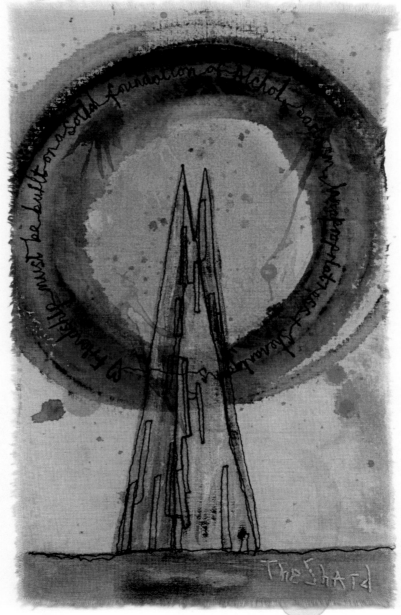

The Shard

This week saw two of my friend's birthdays. It's been a very very long time since I went on a drink fuelled afternoon out. In fact, I don't recall ever doing one without having a drink until now. I had such a laugh, proper belly laughing fun even without the drink. I was the only sober one. I didn't miss it at all and when we all decided to go home, it was like herding cats. Everyone everywhere laughing hard. I had genuinely forgotten what proper belly laughing, naughty cheeky, behaviour you get up to when you have had a few or not as in my case in point. But also, the consequences that come with having too much of a good thing.

But when all said and done, I had such fun. Just being part of a group of funny, inappropriate, entertaining set of people all afternoon, made me feel so good. It made my whole week; I can't live without these people in my life. I love you.

NB: As I reflect whilst writing this I have a question. My question is, why when people drink to excess it is funny, hilarious and amusing? But with food people just find you greedy, glutenous and self-indulgent. What a warped world I live in, everything to excess is fun except for food?

'Friendship must be built on a solid foundation of alcohol, sarcasm, inappropriateness and shenanigans!'

44. 'Ariella'

'Just believe in yourself, even if you don't,
pretend that you do, and, at some point you will.'

Revision is a pain in the butt for sure, we all did it, we all have to do it, but it really is a struggle for my daughter and people like her.

She sits her first round of her iGCSE mocks this week and I reflect back on my own revision. In a world of subjects, struggling what to revise, how to remember vital information, or enough to get by. It's hard really hard especially if you have ADHD brain like ours, that jumps all over the place, reading bits and forgetting it straight away. Trying to put a square peg in a round hole. Finding our way in the world where everything pivots around the results of just a few subjects. Trying to revise in a world that is punitive to so many people like us. So young too. Especially when all our adult life is based on what we perform in our 16th year of life. Why is maths and English so important, why not art, music and drama? Why is everything up to the age of 16 based on these two subjects alone. Its incomprehensible. What if you learn differently? What if there were better ways to get information from people? There must be. I love my girl and all I want for her is to be happy and do what she loves, get a job with what she loves doing and enjoy herself whilst she does it. Come on Ariella you can do this.

45.
'You Decide'

'One day? Or day one, you decide?'

When is the right time to start something new?
One day or is it day One. I think about this a lot
with lots of things. This week it's about exercise.
Currently, I walk the dogs for 20 minutes round
the field opposite our house first thing in a
morning. But I would like to walk longer. It's
still too dark to go earlier... The dogs tend to
find things in the dark and run off. Some
mornings I look out and say, no today I'll do it...
Then reality sets in, it's too cold, I don't want
to get up or it's pouring down with rain.
I'm not winters biggest fan as it is. Some
mornings I literally just lay in bed not wanting
to get up at all, distracted by my phone. This is
my procrastinating side. My thoughtful side
where my mind just wanders off somewhere else
and then I suddenly realise I could have gone
out for longer and now it's too late. This is why
sometimes I'm my own worst enemy. Walking early
is really the best part of the day, but getting my
backside motivated in the winter gets harder and
harder. And so the cycle begins again so, one day?
Or day one'... You decide!

This appreciation is me, head down
deep in thought!

46. 'Majestic'

'It's all about finding calm in the chaos.'

Another week of feeling unwell. Before the covid epidemic I was very rarely physically ill. I could count on one hand how many 'sick' days I'd had in 20 years as a teacher. But since then, every cold type illness seems to floor me. Everything at school this half term ramps up and is manic yet I feel awful. A high temperature, feeling rundown and tired and generally full of cold. The guilt of being ill at school is massive for me too. Leaving my classes with a cover teacher, having my colleagues who are feeling just as stressed as me covering my lessons and then to top it off having to set cover work even when I'm ill. I'd much rather teach my classes then set the work. If I'm too ill to work, cover work is still work. I can't even think straight let alone find something not practical related for the children to do. It makes me feel weak as a person. At times, every now and again, memories of the horrible time covid gave us rears its ugly head and sends me flash backs of how close I was to losing the plot. Reversing all my hard work I have achieved to overcome this. And I have to talk to myself and take a breath, find the calm in the chaos again and move forwards.

47. 'Discipline'

'The pain of discipline is far less
than the pain of regret.'

I still have a million things to do at school and I also
need to make my business work. To make money and sell
more artwork. To get people to come to the shop and see it
as a shop as well as a working space. If I work harder it
will begin to pay off, I read a great book once 'steal like
an artist' by Austin Kleon. It's a book that has helped
me find ideas and not feel guilty by looking at others
work for inspiration. I search Pinterest and I find
images that I need, and I amend them to make them mine,
especially when I'm tired or need inspiration fast.
What I need is my own twist on them to make them mine.
This book has given me the discipline needed, without
the guilt to have made a piece of art every week for
52 weeks. It's like drawing from a photo of a famous
building. Do you need permission from the architect to
copy it? Are portraits of people theirs because it's a picture
of them? No, so it's not cheating drawing your own version of
something. Most ideas are all paintings on paper, board or canvas
yet all mine are in Textiles. A completely different medium all
together to any I have found. Some professionals argue that
textiles is not art anyway its craft. But I beg to differ! Just
by physically making the art for this book has disciplined
me far more than the regret of not doing something in my 50th
year. Friends and family are quite surprised that I've been so
consistent. But here is a woman who has pushed herself out of her
comfort zone again and again to prove herself. Making each piece
of art has made me feel so much better mentally, stronger than I
have been for years and the reality that it's nearly a year and
it will stop soon, fills me with pride and fear at the same time.
I don't want it to end. It's given me purpose to the week.
Its help me navigate some real dark times. The end is scary
yet strangely comforting.

Discipline

101

48.
'Love'

Family being loved no matter what ♡

LOVE

'Family – being loved no matter what!'

What does Christmas mean anyway? Being with family is very important at this time of year, especially over the past few Christmases with 'COVID' hanging over our heads restricting whether we see each other or not. My family are spread far and wide and this is one time where we do try to come together at least once every 2 years. This year I'm not organised at all, I am not feeling it, it took me three weeks to put decorations on my tree and even then, it was only lights. I just don't feel Christmassy at all. My partner's really poorly, so he didn't come with us to Yorkshire, my dad has just been diagnosed with vascular dementia and my sister and her family are all still in Dubai. All that being said, it still was a really lovely Christmas. Calm, gentle, little fuss and full of love. Yet again my appreciation puts everything into perspective, grounds me once again and makes me appreciate what I have. That I don't need to spend a fortune and travel thousands of miles to make everything just perfect. Just seeing my close family and friends is everything and more that I have and need right now.

49. 'To Fly'

The bird that dares to fall
is the bird who learns
to fly

That song lyric by Chumbawamba 'I get knocked down, but I get up again, you never gonna keep me down...' it came out when I was at University in the 90's and it has been my theme tune ever since. It means no matter how many times I fail or am knocked down or back, I should always stand strong, brush the dust off and carry on. I used to physically fall down a lot too. This morning I watched a bird fly straight into my patio doors, play dead for a couple of seconds and then get up, shake off and fly away. I often sit and watch the birds and wonder what it would be like to be able to fly? Seeing the bird fly into the window and get back up again and carry on like nothing ever happened, reminded me of that song and contemplate life again. Liking it to being on a roller coaster ride waiting for it to stop, when it stops not knowing what to do and then staying on it for another go in case it changes. I could learn a lot from a bird and its simple life.

'The bird that dares to fall is the bird who learns to fly'

50. 'Protection'

'It's easier to be brave when your child needs your protection'

I have never experienced anything like the rage inside me when someone hurts my daughter. It's like something possesses me and takes over me from the inside. Turns me into this foreign being that will do anything to protect what is mine. The lioness and her cub can be compared to a mother and her child in that they both demonstrate unconditional love, protection, and support for one another. The lioness is fiercely protective of her cub and goes to great lengths to nurture and guide them. I will always put her needs before my own when she needs me. Nothing else matters around me until it is solved or I have exhausted every single avenue to try and get what she needs. Everything I do is to give this precious child of mine opportunities, happiness, and growth.

I'm sure I'm not on my own here. But if I am then no matter what I will continue doing so until the day comes where she no longer needs me to. I will protect and defend her until my last breath.

51. 'Unworthy'.

one of the hardest battles we fight
is between what we know and
what we feel ♡

This week I am left feeling very insecure. I know people buy my work, that I'm quite a good painter. I know this because even people I don't know sometimes buy it. But there are times, only sometimes, when even I doubt my own ability. I doubt that my art is any good, why do I get rejected from art sites, why people don't buy at shows. I ask myself, why don't I sell more? what is wrong with me? It can be, if I let it get hold of me, like a rabbit hole, like the one I used to live down. It's probably why I love Alice-in-Wonderland so much. I can't help it. Those self-sabotaging thoughts that spiral out of control. A good friend once bought me a mug and on it was written – 'The creative process = wow it's amazing – I'm not sure – this is s*** – I am s*** – oh it might work – Wow it's amazing' and so on and so forth in a circle going round and round and round. That is just like it is to be me. This is what it's like being alive, welcome to the world Kate. AGAIN!

'One of the hardest battles we fight is between what we know and what we feel.'

52. 'The Gift'

'The meaning of life is to find your gift –
The purpose of life is to give it away.'

So, here it is, the last appreciation. A cupcake with a single candle in it. Symbolising ONE whole year of Appreciations. I am using a quote by William Shakespeare 'The meaning of life is to find your gift, the purpose of life is to give it away!' My gift is Art. Here I am laid raw and bare showing you that you too could do the same. I think that's why I am, and love being a teacher and an Artist. I have knowledge, I have skills, I have love, and I have empathy in spades, for the children that I have taught and are still to teach.

I emphatically believe that every single person can be an artist no matter their ability as long as they are true to themselves and their beliefs. In fact, they can be whomever they wish to be in life full stop.

My one wish from blowing out the candle, is for everyone to believe in themselves just a smidge more. A bit like the mug that I talked about last week why do we doubt our own capabilities, we are all so much more capable than we think we are.

What's next?!

I'm putting it out there again,
what's next for me ...

Get in touch via social

@ katetulettart

email: katetulettart@gmail.com

SCAN ME